HAPPY BIRTHDAY, MRS. PRESIDENT

Finesse Literary Press Edition

By
Ben Simon Lazarus

Published by Finesse Literary Press
http://www.finesseliterarypress.com

Copyright 2020

All rights reserved. No part of this publication may be reproduced, stored in a retrieval system or transmitted in any form or by any means, electronic, mechanical, photocopy, recording or otherwise, without prior written consent of the copyright owner. Nor can it be circulated in any form of binding or cover other than that in which it is published and without similar condition including this condition being imposed on a subsequent purchaser.

The right of Ben Simon Lazarus to be identified as the author of this work has been asserted in accordance with the Copyright Designs and Patents Act 1988.

A copy of this book is deposited with the British Library

Table of Contents

Epilogue 5
Chapter 1 7
Chapter 2 12
Chapter 3 17
Chapter 4 22
Chapter 5 27
Chapter 6 33
Chapter 7 39
Chapter 8 44
Chapter 9 48
Chapter 10 53
Chapter 11 58
Chapter 12 63

Epilogue

The situation room is empty, except for me. The Marine who carried today's football lies unconscious near the door. I'm certain he would stop me, if he had the chance. He's a good Marine. His name is Curtis Brimmer, thirty-something. He has one of those smiles you see in the movies, white teeth and a hint of danger. He'll be blamed for what is about to happen, and that's too bad. But someone has to be blamed for the nuking of London and Paris, and, well, a lot of big cities. ICBMs aren't just for Russia and China anymore. I have the codes in front of me, and, while we're at DEFCON 5, that doesn't mean I can't launch ground, air, and sea assets. The recipients of our largesse will be totally surprised. Hell, the entire world will be surprised. The poor souls in New York, Los Angeles, and here in DC will be more than just surprised. When the retaliation happens, they'll be dead.

Like me.

People think that right before death, their life will flash before their eyes. That's not true for me. My past marches through my brain constantly. I remember the bad things mostly. That's human nature. We focus on the bad, so we don't repeat bad behavior. The good doesn't need to be remembered, although for most of us, there isn't that much good. In terms of bandwidth alone, it would be more efficient to remember the good. Nope. We hug the bad and feel embarrassed over and over again. It's a form of self-punishment. It's the source of most of my wishes. I wish so much that things hadn't turned out the way they did. I'm guessing that in a few minutes, the blokes in England and the compadres in Mexico City will feel the same.

DEFCON 5

The world at peace.

The only real war is inside me. How the hell did that happen?

Chapter 1

Mom abandoned me for the first time when I was seven. I didn't know she abandoned me. All I knew was that my dad started fixing my breakfast before school. That was mom's job, and she did a better job than dad, who put a box of fruit loops, milk, bowl, and spoon on the table. He was efficient, if not exactly cognizant of what I liked to eat. Then, again, he never ate breakfast with me. He sometimes would sip coffee and talk to mom while I was there, but sitting down and talking school stuff? That must have caused him pain, because he never did it. He was smart enough to turn on the TV—cartoons—before he disappeared into his home office. At seven, I was more than responsible enough to rinse out my bowl and load the dishwasher. Dad would reappear just before the yellow school bus picked me up.

"Be good. Work hard."

He said the same thing every morning, as if I might forget. I had a good memory, and I told him so. It made no difference.

"Be good. Work hard."

It was maybe a week before I asked about mom. Dad said she was on vacation and would return in another week or two or three. Dad wasn't specific about mom. No one was. She was a force all by herself. I knew she had good days and bad days because of my clothes. One day, my closet would be stuffed with clean and ironed skirts, jeans, pants, tops, all the clothes a little girl could need. It was exactly like the fridge. One day filled with good things to eat. Then, nothing for days on end. The closet, like the fridge, became bare. And it wasn't as if mom wasn't home. She was. But for some reason, the cooking and cleaning and washing didn't happen regularly. Sometimes, I had to remind her that I was running out of underwear. That usually stoked the fire, but not always.

When mom returned that first time, it was Christmas in February. The closet and fridge were always full. I ate pancakes, my favorite, every morning. School was actually fun, and I didn't hear "Be good. Work hard." once. The good, new days. I think dad was pretty happy too. I caught him smiling on two occasions. Those perfect weeks flashed by. Then, mom left again.

The era of fruit loops and macaroni arrived. I had settled in for the long days of sugar and food from a box, when dad struck it rich. I wasn't quite sure what he did, but he was good at it. Because, while mom was "away", dad hired a housekeeper and a gardener and an au pair. I had no idea what an au pair was, but pancakes for breakfast and clean clothes were fine with me. The au pair had her room, and she stayed there mostly, except for the nights when she crept into dad's room. I had no idea what that was about, and as long as the new clothes and toys arrived, I didn't care. The au pair was the only person dad didn't yell at—and that included me.

"Be good. Work hard."

I always thought the Advisors came with the au pair. I mean, they showed up at the same time. I don't remember when I started calling them "advisors". I do remember when one of my dolls, Smelly-Nelly, spoke to me. Her lips didn't move, but I heard the voice plain as day, one of those whiny voices from TV. Smelly-Nelly talked to me about Saylor, a boy at school who thought it great fun to pinch people. He especially like to pinch me. Sure, the teacher spoke to Saylor about it, but her gentle pleadings didn't work. He would nod and promise and pinch someone on the way to his desk. I met a lot of Saylors later in life, and they were all assholes.

"The next time Saylor pinches you," Smelly-Nelly said, "you take your ruler and smack his nose…hard."

Now, I had been steeped in non-physical responses to pinchers, and name-callers, and trippers, and all the types that existed on the playground. No one had ever told me to haul off and nail someone. So, Smelly-Nelly's advice rang true. The next time Saylor pinched my arm, I grabbed my ruler and smacked him. How was I to know that his nose would bleed, and he would cry like a baby? The teacher gave Saylor a tissue to try and rescue his already ruined shirt and hustled him to the nurse. The other kids just stared at me.

The Saylor mission cost me recess for two weeks. Dad sat me down for a thirty second talk that included an "Atta girl" for showing initiative. Still, I had to promise that I wouldn't do it again. Thinking back on the episode, the price paid was not too high. Saylor never pinched me again, and neither did anyone else. Enough said. In the decades after, I longed for that ruler. It might have saved me a lot of anguish.

Smelly-Nelly was soon joined by Steady-Eddy, Risky-Randy, and Nosey-Nora. Those weren't the names of the dolls. I made them up because of the tips they gave me. In the long years before I knew anything of Yin and Yang, I recognized the value of listening to opposing views. My Advisors never lacked for ideas and spirited discussion. Like any Captain of the ship, I heeded the advice I found useful. The rest went the way of the trash can.

When mom returned the second time, I expected an end to pancakes and fresh clothes. I was wrong. Everyone stayed in place. Mom spent her time mostly by the pool, looking at nothing particularly and getting regular pills from the au pair. I was too young to figure out what was going on. All I knew was that mom rarely laughed or kissed me on the forehead. I was getting too old for that any way. Life seemed pretty good to me. If mom suffered, I didn't see it. She didn't yell any more or cry for that matter. Lost in my own little world with my Advisors, I focused on the things that made me happy—clothes, toys, and TV.

"Be good. Work hard."

I pretty much figured the au pair forgot mom's pills on purpose. I didn't know if dad had instructed the au pair. Not that it mattered. The end result was perfectly predictable. Mom went nuts. That she didn't break every piece of crystal in the house was because dad had the foresight to lock the cabinet where the most expensive items were kept. Foresight or plan? I never knew. Mom went away for the third time, and dad sat me down for the "big talk". Like most adults, he figured that a very young girl didn't need much in the way of information.

"Your mother is ill and is in the hospital," dad said.

"When is she coming home?"

"I don't know. When she gets better."

"Can I go visit?"

"In time, in time. For now, be good—"

"Work hard," I finished.

Dad laughed at that. Since he never laughed often, I was pleased.

Soon after that, that au pair moved on, replaced by another girl of the same ilk and same habits. Dad must have done all right in business, because he was always buying me gifts and clothes. Until I was ten, I thought part of the au pair's job was the nocturnal visit to dad's bedroom. After ten, I sort of figured out the lay of the land, so to speak. That was when dad transferred me to the Christian Academy, a place with strict rules and stricter uniforms. The school being all girls, I was lost for a while. Then, one of the tribe befriended the "newbie". I learned more in one month with Monica than I learned in all my previous years. More than half of what she told me proved to be wrong, but it sure sounded right at the time. The plaid skirt, white blouse, knee-high socks, and saddles must have done something for me. Because when dad took me to a filming of him in a commercial, the director took one look at me and pushed me into the ad.

"She's perfect," the director said.

Chapter 2

On the way home, dad grinned. If the commercial worked, I was booked for several more. I would be the innocent little schoolgirl of a million different fantasies. Several more commercials rolled out. Dad's business soared. I became the "it" schoolgirl. Halloween costume makers mimicked my uniform. At the time, I had no idea there was a schoolgirl trope that played through society. I would soon learn.

My father liked to think that pushing me into show business was his idea. I was pretty sure the au pair suggested that I would make a good spokesperson for a number of enterprises. Dad became my manager and enrolled me in all manner of after-school classes. I studied elocution and movement and accents and method acting, anything that dad thought would enhance my career as the schoolgirl everyone dreamed about. The director called me his little "gold mine". The money poured in, and dad bought me even more stuff. When I went to the mall, people would say "hey", especially the old fogies who thought a wink would tell me something. It didn't. But I didn't know just how popular I was until the girls at school started shunning me. That was the tipoff. The clique couldn't abide my fame.

The Advisors took my side and told me to follow the money. Money would lead to fame, and fame would lead to more money. If there was a panacea for all problems, it was money.

As long as I remembered that, I would do just fine. If my grades suffered, so be it. If my school popularity suffered, so much the better. I had more time to study acting. I was in a win-win situation, as far as the Advisors were concerned. Of course, when the au pair caught me talking to the Advisors, dad became an issue—until I assured him that I was merely practicing my pronunciation and accents. That earned me an extra pair of Birkenstocks. Dad was never one for deep conversations.

High school arrived and with it the throes of dating. The au pair (I forget which one exactly) was my source of advice for dating. The Advisors simply weren't equipped to guide me through the maze of puberty hormones. Best friends came and went on a regular basis. The make-out party became the weekend activity of choice. Learning how to fend off boys who seemed to have more appendages than an octopus was a skill that required more than a few repetitions to get perfect. Luckily, the first time I tried smoking, I almost choked to death, and my initiation to alcohol cost me the lining of my stomach—or so it felt. In any case, I developed an ironclad rule. No drugs, no alcohol. The rule allowed me to survey the damage caused to my friends. The first funeral I attended made the girl seem special. Two days later, my classmates couldn't remember the color of her eyes. Death didn't endear anyone to anyone.

Then, in junior year, I met Peter.

Peter was as handsome as a C-list movie star. He was sensitive, as jocks went, and his friend was Larry Monk, who had scholarship offers from three Division I colleges. That made Larry the best athlete in the school. The three of us would meet in the library to study, which generally meant an hour of tutoring Larry so he could maybe pass Freshman math, and an hour making out with Peter and allowing him more liberties than all the other boys combined. It was a wonderful time that climaxed in the Spring Fling, the formal dance where every guy wore a tux and ever girl a tiara. It was love, pure love. I knew then that Peter and I were destined to be together. Magic does that. Some people are unforgettable. Peter was one of them. Even after I moved to California.

The director was my ticket to Los Angeles. His commercials (starring me) led to a movie gig. He wasn't there a month before he called dad. There seemed to be a dearth of special schoolgirls in California, where the "valley girls" wouldn't be caught dead in a school uniform. Dad was only too happy to oblige the director. We didn't even wait for the semester break. I packed my uniforms and flew to the coast with Dad and my Advisors. I had to leave the actual dolls at home, but by that time, I could conjure up the Advisors any time I wanted.

If commercials were the only work for me in Los Angeles, we wouldn't have moved. But the director got a sitcom gig that was perfect for everyone's favorite schoolgirl. The money was good. The parties and drugs better. Dad was in his element, sunglasses at midnight and sleep till noon. I went to school. I studied acting, public speaking, persuasion, and rhetoric. I could talk a cat into barking. To top it all off, Peter and I stayed in love, probably because we didn't see very much of each other. If he cheated, I never knew. I did know that dad liked Peter and urged me to keep Peter in the mix. It wasn't until dad caught Peter and me in bed together that dad laid down the law. Peter was going to wed America's favorite schoolgirl, and that was all there was to it.

We made it happen. The month after our separate-but-equal graduations, dad walked me down the aisle. Yes, he wore sunglasses (Hollywood), and yes, he did give me away (sort of). After a rather fabulous two weeks in Hawaii, Peter and I returned to the Beverly Hills mansion. Dad cruised in overdrive. Peter discovered his vocation was lounging about the pool with several "valley girls". I was chained to the sitcom and several minor movie roles that took me on location for a week at a time. I was still the clever schoolgirl, but I had added the vapid teenager destined to be murdered first in a horror movie. I didn't know if that was moving up or moving out. Still, things were rolling until dad fell walking down a stairway in a major hotel. Yep, sunglasses at midnight. The hospital claimed him for ten days. During that ten days, I hired another manager to negotiate a contract. He brought along an accountant. The accountant was a good one, much to dad's chagrin. It turned out dad had been siphoning off millions to fund his sunglasses, habits, and some rather ill-advised investments in the Nevada desert. That was enough to send me over the edge. I couldn't wait for him to come home. There would be a reckoning.

The coward dodged his day in my court.

I was shooting an episode when dad went to the garage, started his Mercedes, and forgot to open the garage door. He died, even as Peter worked on his tan. I found dad. That night, I sent Peter packing. I had found my last pair of valley-girl panties under the bed. Oddly, Peter begged to stay. I supposed none of the valley girls wanted someone without a dime. Not oddly, I shoved Peter out the door without even a car. And being without a car in LA was akin to a death sentence. I didn't care. I was more than a bit pissed.

I buried dad and mourned the usual amount of time for an LA denizen—three days. When I walked back on the set, the director I had made into a staple in Hollywood took me aside.

"Good news and bad news," he said.

Chapter 3

I had memorized any number of "good news/bad news" lines from the sitcom. I thought I knew them all. Yet, he surprised me.

"The good news is you're out of the show. The bad news is I got a new, better show."

"Wait," I said. "How is that good news for me and bad news for you?"

"You are now free to pursue your career in film, something I always thought you wanted. While I am chained to the wheel of weekly TV. I must stifle my ambition."

"Oh, I get it," I said. "I am now unemployed and broke, since my father stole all my money. While you are employed and living like some Medieval king."

He shook his head. "You forget that Medieval kings lived in drafty, old castles that were hot in the summer, cold in the winter, and infested with vermin all year long. No one in his right mind would want to live like that."

"Tell that to the homeless. Oh, wait, the homeless aren't in their right minds, are they?"

"Look, you know how this business goes. One day, you're riding the wave, the next you're wiped out. In your case, bad press was the anchor. It dragged you right to the bottom. My advice is to give your career some time to resurface. Everybody loves a comeback story. You're primo material. I'll write the screenplay myself. Midwestern transplant rises from the ashes like a Phoenix. How do you like it?"

"You touch one day of my story, and I'll sue your ass till you can't sit. Got that?"

I left the director laughing. He knew I didn't have the chops to sue him, not for anything. In Hollywood, some people were untouchable—until they weren't. I would have to bide my time.

I managed to keep the Beverly Hills property by renting out the mansion and assigning myself to the guest cottage. My agreement stipulated that I had to be out of the cottage by seven AM (if I was going to leave) and home after eight PM. The renters had no desire to see a washed-up, sitcom, schoolgirl going back and forth while they enjoyed the pool and the glorious California sun. I didn't mind. I wasn't going anywhere anyway. My mind and body had entered into some sort of cocoon phase. I didn't leave the cottage. My daily meal of ramen noodles always arrived after eight PM. Luckily, I had laid in a store of cheap wine. Wine and ramen noodles by candlelight was just the thing. The firelight drew forth the Advisors, like moths to a flame.

It was during those wine-soaked hours that my childhood Advisors transformed into their adult version. They came with new names.

LAURENT: a middle-aged man who chronicled and categorized my worst instincts and desires. After dad, Peter, and the director, I had a brain full of horrible desires.

MATTHEW: a young man of earnest mien, whose job it was to keep me safe and operational. Matthew wouldn't let me cross the street without looking four ways, including up.

TRISDA: a young girl who could double as Gandhi. She loved every living creature and most of the dead ones. She would forgive her executioner.

ARTHUR: a young boy who couldn't really exist, as he possessed the wisdom of Solomon. He was forever making lists and demonstrating with geometric logic the folly of my ways.

THE MATRON: an older woman who reminded me of Two-Face, a nemesis of Batman. The Matron was half dad, half mom, and she could be as cruel and nice as those two at their worst. Her advice always involved money.

Surrounded by my Advisors, I delved into the wine-induced musings of my future. Since no producers or directors had called, and my agent no longer returned my texts, I was forced to assume that my acting career had come to a four-wheel-disc-brake stop. I was going nowhere in Hollywood. Facing that truth prepared me for life back in the Midwest, but that wasn't really a life. I considered it a form of suspended animation. Almost life but not really. I wasn't going back. The Advisors pointed to the future.

What future?

That was the real question. What was a washed-out sitcom star equipped to do? The answer really wasn't so difficult to surmise. The Advisors recognized it right away. I could act, which meant I could lie. In fact, I could lie better than most. Ergo, my future lay in exactly one sphere—

Politics.

While my training and skills shouted "POLITICS", my natural bent was toward truth. Laurent and The Matron quickly disabused me of that notion. Truth was the last thing a politician wanted to spout. No, the truth would only confuse the masses of people who were more interested in the latest Netflix offering than in sound policies. To reach my natural level of incompetence, I would have to appeal to the largest strata of voters. Those would be the people who still believed they controlled their lives. The American promise of liberty and freedom stirred the hearts of these faithful, who were too blind to see how big government and big business controlled the levers of power. The truth would get me a small cadre of fanatics, but it would not propel me into the national limelight. For that, I would have to become St. Schoolgirl, the government-dragon slayer. I would also need to promise "Fortress-America", a realm no immigrants could invade.

The road to success started with a blog. During those long hours of wine and ramen twilight zones, I became the All-America Schoolgirl, dedicated to truth, justice and the effing American way. Matthew didn't always approve of my twisted logic, but he was invaluable when it came to explaining the chimerical benefits of trickle-down economics. I knew the truth of trickle-down everything. But I had to feed my readers and supporters the red meat of the American dream. Yes, they too could have their own sitcom—if only they listened to me. I was the voice in the wilderness, the guru on the mountain, Uncle Samantha in schoolgirl tartan. I had the face, the chops, the voice, the lies everyone wanted to hear. I claimed to be an independent, but I trended Republican. Actually, the blog was pure Libertarian, but Laurent wisely told me that Libertarians were the lost tribe of politics. Everyone agreed with them. No one voted for them.

I lined up with the Republican candidate for president. He was only too happy to have me warm up the crowd before he took the stage. I whipped the faithful into a frenzy. Had I been Joan of Arc, I could have led them into Paris to claim the arche de triomphe for the red, white, and blue. According to the political savants of the press and Internet, I was the headliner. The candidate was weak-as-skim-milk follow up. The crowds left the arenas chanting my name, not his. The networks picked up my speeches, altering their coverage. The schoolgirl had come of age. I did everything in my power to push the insipid candidate over the top.

And I failed.

The race was decided on election night.

My candidate had lost.

I had won.

That was when the Advisors rushed to the fore. I had established myself as a formidable icon for the dreams of non-historians. I had taken "America" off the lists of banned words. Yet, the Advisors reminded me that modern voters forgot everything in a week, maybe two. If I were going to advance my political career, I needed to stay in the game. I needed to put my face front and center every night. I needed to reinforce my "savior" image. I needed to slay more dragons and lead the people to the promised land—and that wasn't Canada.

The first thing I had to do was repair my image.

Chapter 4

Besides giving me a megaphone and a direct connection to the umpteen millions of disgruntled voters, the campaign refilled my coffers. I once again had money, which allowed me to end the lease and kick out the bitches who had made my life miserable. Since I was popular, the networks scheduled me for all the Sunday, politics shows and many of the news channels. I found myself presenting my utterly unprocessed drivel to millions of viewers. The schoolgirl had grown up, and she had the eye and ear of the populace. In other words, I was a hit. That put more money in the bank. It also allowed Laurent to tell me to get my husband back.

Single men and women are rarely elected to high office.

I might have argued with Laurent, had I known any history. But I didn't, so I took his word for it. If I wanted to move into lawful theft, I would have to find a husband.

Peter should do. It would help if you can somehow manage to add a couple of children.

"Peter cheated on me," I reminded Laurent. "That doesn't make me real anxious to get him back."

It doesn't have to be a union, just a marriage. Tell him he can have the good life as long as he toes the line. He's handsome enough, glib enough. He can be an asset, with some coaching.

Laurent made perfect sense, but I still didn't want to follow it. I no longer needed Peter, not in any marital way. I needed him if I wanted to get elected, and I sorely wanted to get elected. I had seen how the other side lived, their private jets and free everything. People lined up to do a favor or give away money. I had been shocked in the beginning, but I was no longer shocked. I was shockproof. No among of depravity or theft surprised me. I had dipped my toe into the river Bacchanal, and I liked the feel of silk. While I still thought of Hollywood stars as pampered and privileged, they were servants compared to politicians. Who had more money than the government?

No one.

That was a lesson well learned. And he who had the money had the power. That was the second lesson. If the love of money was the root of all evil, then the government was Satan and Lucifer and every demon ever invented rolled into one. Money. I had lived with it, and I had lived without it. I had promised myself that I would never live without it again.

I found Peter in a bar on Miami Beach. He didn't look too bad, and the older woman he was with sort of made it clear that he was some sort of gigolo. I had to admit that the older woman was well preserved and was obviously rich, two qualities gigolos depended upon. Yet, the woman was no match for me. It took but one hour to convince Peter that he could ride the starship SCHOOLGIRL right to the end of the universe. All he had to do was be at my side when needed and extremely discreet when he wasn't at my side. If he wanted to learn to play golf or sail boats, fine. He just couldn't get caught with his pants down. That would toss him off the gravy train. He would be condemned to charming old ladies out of booze money.

Peter proved he could master any role. He played the doting husband to a tee. Neither one of us wanted to toss children into the mix. We were both too selfish. I was afraid The Matron would take over and turn the kids into little robots without souls. That's what my parents did to me. I wasn't aware of it at the time, but I had learned. There wasn't a lot of depth to me. That hurt in the beginning, but it was perfect for politics. I could embrace an eco-warrior for breakfast, a coal miner for lunch, and a gun enthusiast for dinner. All I had to do was memorize some lines. I was good at that. And I had to look like a schoolgirl. That was even easier. I was a natural, and therefore, a danger to the people who already occupied the seats of power.

You must find a niche. You must find an unoccupied lane you can own. Look around, choose the not-so-popular policies and adopt them.

When I looked at the political Interstate, I found way too many crowded lanes, filled with people who actually believed part of the prattle they fed their constituents. So, I looked to the outside lanes, the ones close to the berm, to being off the road altogether. If socialists crowded a lane, I became antisocialist. When liberals vied for the center lane, I moved to the antiliberal lane. The elite and the media raced in their own lanes, so I raced in the anti-lanes. Since every politician I met believed in government, I became a heretic. No big government for me. When the movers and shakers badmouthed the working class, I championed them. I told the audience that they would have pry my gun from my cold, dead hands. Whenever I ran into some kind of glitch, I called upon the shadow world of conspiracy. Nothing was ever my fault. Someone, somewhere, somehow had ruined things.

Ordinary people loved it.

When someone from the crowd yelled, "Clear the swamp!", I promised on a Bible to clean out the creatures that made life hell for the rest of us. When someone asked a question about taxes, I shouted back, "TOO DAMN HIGH!". That always brought down the house. I didn't know if I believed half of what I said. It didn't matter. I had been trained to make people believe, even when they knew better. That was my job, and I was damn good at it. I hired some political types who put together the PACs and support groups, who ushered me from one $10,000-per-plate dinner to the next. If I promised an oil pipeline to one group, I promised a gas pipeline to the next. I owned that far right lane, the one everyone else abandoned. Fine with me. I knew it was better to own it all than to share it with a bunch of other parasites.

That was how I became a Senator, which was tantamount to becoming a demigod. The richest men and women in the world bowed and groveled and donated—as long as I promised not to come after their corporations and savings. Being one of the very, very elite, the most powerful one hundred humans since Rome, that was nearly the tallest mountain in the world. My backers were immensely happy. They didn't realize that from my perch, I still had to look up. When you're as close as a Senator, scaling that last mountain looks like a walk in the park. I knew it wouldn't be, but I was determined to get there. I wasn't exactly sure why. I guess, it was because all my Advisors told me that I wouldn't sleep at night if I didn't snooze under the presidential seal.

Did I believe that?

It didn't matter.

My Advisors believed it, and they were willing to pay any price (me), for the privilege of selling the Lincoln bedroom to the highest bidder.

That was why Laurent came up with my catch phrase.

CHAPTER 5

MAKE AMERICA WONDERFUL AGAIN

I registered the phrase with the patent office even before I started campaigning for the next level. Of course, that started my rather furious dispute with the framers of the US Constitution. In the infinite stupidity, they included age requirements for both senators and president. While I qualified for the Senate, I was several years shy of qualifying for the oval office. Perhaps age was a factor way back when, but modern members of society grew up far faster than before. I considered myself as wise as Jefferson or Madison. After all, they had never enjoyed the advantages of the Internet. I could learn more in a day than they could in a year. So, why did I have to wait till the candles on my birthday cake matched the magic number in Article II of the Constitution?

Because a bunch of old men decided that young people had mush for brains. And maybe they did back when steering a wagon was the closest thing they had to an automobile. If I had possessed some sort of time machine, I would have transported Mr. Jefferson to my house and handed him the keys to the Porsche. Let's see how that plantation knowledge worked in the realm of hundred-mile-per-hour travel. I was willing to bet that he would crash on the first go around.

So, why did I have to wait?

I considered ignoring the law and mounting a protest campaign. My popularity was soaring, so I considered my chances of winning pretty good. Then, Arthur, the logician Arthur, reminded me that there were nine people in black robes whose sole goal in life was ensuring that everyone, everyone followed the Constitution. Since they were all much older and rather stuck in their ways, I knew I would be blown out of the water before I left port. Arthur was also quick to remind me that people who failed in their first attempt to win the white house often didn't get another attempt. The Matron counseled patience, something I wasn't blessed with. Still, I did have a certain amount of self-control. No actor could succeed without self-control. Step out of character for an instant, and the director screams "cut" and reads you the riot act for pronouncing Dixie without the requisite Southern drawl. I would weather the years I had to wait. My Advisors convinced me to use the time to build the MAWA machine.

For a nano-second, I considered using Peter to design and equip the MAWA army. I considered it an army, because I would need a lot of worker bees if I were going to win. Then, I remembered Patton, the movie. When I compared Peter to Patton, Peter came up more than a little short. There was no way in hell Peter could find and train the people I needed. Peter couldn't even speak Southern, their preferred language. No, Peter would have to play First Gentleman, charming the ladies and drinking Scotch with the men. Peter did have some skills. Trisda actually felt sorry for Peter, but then Trisda felt sorry for cockroaches too.

In actuality, the Advisors became my generals. They provided the blueprints and bylaws for my following. I couldn't call them an army, and I certainly couldn't equip them as one—

although, I would have loved a few snipers at my beck and call. Putting up with a bunch of smelly, old Senators was not my idea of a fun time. Still, there were plenty of political junkies who would work for the highest dollar. They were whores, whose allegiance was to the greenback. Laurent made that abundantly clear. They were loyal to whoever paid them best. The Praetorian Guard couldn't have been more mercenary. I had to keep tabs on all of them, to the point where I monitored their cell phones without their knowledge. The first time they talked to the opposition, I sent them packing. Well, not me so much, as Laurent. He hated Benedict Arnolds. I always meant to have him explain Benedict Arnold to me, but I never got the chance.

In the greater scheme of my plan to conquer, my Advisors made most of the decisions, and they worked for free. They chose my merchandiser, the person in charge of manufacturing and distributing my MAWA shirts, hats, pants, flags, license plates, bumper stickers, pins, and underwear. I had to admit that the panties were quite attractive, and on the right woman promised a night to remember. Well, I hoped they did. The Advisors also chose my data guru, the guy with thick-lens glasses who lived in some underground bunker in the middle of fly-over country. That guy knew the name, age, shoe size, and favorite TV show of every voter both alive and dead. Laurent told me to never ignore the value of the dead voter. In some cities, the dead formed their own voting bloc. I added state co-ordinators and city coordinators and precinct coordinators, more coordinators than could possibly be needed. When I worried about the money flying out of the campaign coffers, Laurent simply shrugged. I had to spend money to make money. I wasn't sure if that was Laurent or Dad who said that. Didn't matter. On my thirty-fifth birthday, I was in control of the best army since the blitzkrieg. I was going to take no prisoners.

When I launched my campaign, I thanked my dead dad for all those years on TV. Where better qualified men and women struggled with name and face recognition, I suffered no such setback. The schoolgirl who had charmed millions of viewers was going to MAKE AMERICA WONDERFUL AGAIN. The banners backed me at every rally. The hats popped up like dandelions in the crowds of enthusiasts. Laurent wrote the speeches, the promises to put god, gun, and country in the education of every little boy and girl in the country. Everybody's favorite schoolgirl was going to storm the citadel of the elite and send the pretenders packing. The swamp would be drained faster than a bodega's register during a stickup. The greatest capitol the world had ever known would once again belong to the people and not the denizens of K-Street. That I promised to disband Congress until they hung a copy of the Ten Commandments in every courthouse and school was a highlight of every rally. The people had had enough of pajama people in onesies. Rugged was the word of the day. We would take no prisoners.

The campaign was long and draining. Luckily, I was the youngest candidate in the field. I made all those pancake breakfasts and burger lunches and fried chicken dinners. My voice didn't get hoarse. I didn't need anyone to help me mount the steps to the stage. I was the picture of health, well, physical health. I kept the Advisors secret, as I didn't believe my admirers would appreciate the round-robin input I received before I made a decision. Laurent was adamant about that. If word leaked out about the Advisors, I would be sent packing. The good old boys didn't put a lot of truck into psychology.

In a way, the campaigning was fun. It was a lot more interesting than reading bills and voting in the Senate. That suited the octo-octogenarians who were my colleagues. It was BORING for anyone who didn't wear an adult diaper. The road was my friend. MAWA was my greeting. My peeps tallied the poll numbers every day. While I rose steadily, I was not the favorite, which I found hard to believe. Who wouldn't vote for America's Schoolgirl? It was the last week, when the dweebs brought me the poll numbers that I slipped into depression. According to the finest pollsters in the universe, I was doomed to lose. All the energy, all the tears, all the sacrifices were for naught. I was doomed to the ash heap of history, the person who didn't win. Whoever remembered that name?

That was when Matthew came to the fore. He reminded me that life wasn't about arriving. It was about the trip. I was having the trip of anyone's lifetime. I was vying to be the most powerful human in the known universe. The end point was bound to be disappointing. After all, it wasn't as if I were going to be Emperor Schoolgirl. The Lilliputians (whoever they were) and swamp creatures would work night and day to shackle me and prevent me from achieving great things. That was the end game. I would never be able to do what I wanted. So, I needed to live in the moment. I needed to immerse myself in the cheers and best wishes of the great unwashed. That was important. The journey held all the grandeur and achievement. If I kept that in mind, I was already the winner.

Of course, Matthew was lying through his teeth. His words sounded great, and I did drop myself into the present. But everyone, everyone knew that losing was the pits. Losing relegated me to the great bin of the unremarkable. I would no longer be

America's Schoolgirl. I would be nobody. And being nobody was the worst thing in the world.

MAKE AMERICA WONDERFUL AGAIN

Those were the last words I pronounced before I settled back with Peter to watch the results. He tried to console me, and he almost succeeded. Things were going decidedly against me when I went to bed. I had already written a congratulations speech that no one would listen to. Still, I was duty-bound to give it.

CHAPTER 6

Peter woke me at four AM with the news.

I had won.

As impossible as that was, it was the absolute truth. Those battleground states that had been predicted to go for my opponent, saw the promise of MAWA and cast their votes for America's Schoolgirl. Not one pundit or political guru called the race correctly. The networks were dumbfounded. In the opposing camp, the recriminations popped up fast and furious. Calls for recounts and protests of fraud filled the airwaves and the online world. The polls couldn't have been that far wrong, could they? I had less chance of winning than Wile E. Coyote. It was the upset of the century, maybe of the millennium. I had been less chance than David vs. Goliath.

Amazing.

So, instead of a capitulation speech. I was rousted out of bed and into campaign headquarters to give my acceptance speech. I thanked my campaign manager, my husband, my workers, my backers, and most of all the people who had gone out and voted for me. In the good, old USA, the votes mattered. I had more than the other guy, so I was now the president-elect. I knew what that meant, but I wasn't at all sure I was prepared to become the most powerful person in the universe. The first thing I needed to get used to was the Secret

Service. While they had hung around during the campaign, they were mostly second teamers. The other guy had the first string. After the election, the first team arrived on my doorstep, all in like suits and carrying like weapons.

The Secret Service gave me my very first briefing.

As far as the Secret Service was concerned, I was not the boss. They were—as far as security was concerned. If they wanted me in the White House bunker, I was going to the bunker. If they wanted to keep me from mingling with the crowd, I wouldn't mingle. If I wanted to stop for a burger and fries, they would vet the place long before I actually arrived. They didn't give a damn about MAWA or America's Schoolgirl. They had orders to keep me alive at any cost. As far as they were concerned, if I died, they would get a black eye, and they didn't want a black eye. By the end of the briefing, I was steamed enough to remind them that they worked at my pleasure, not the other way around. I didn't because Laurent reminded me that being on the outs with the security guards was not the place to be. I tabled my anger for the moment. I would deal with them later.

After that first briefing, all hell broke loose. For some asinine reason, everyone expected me to come up with a cabinet. They acted like I knew all the swamp creatures who needed jobs. The people with fake smiles had been around through any number of administrations, so they had to be competent, if not superior. That was the logic, and it passed Arthur's test. I wasn't sold. If they were so good, why were they begging me for a job. What the swamp creatures were really good at was talking. They talked morning, noon, and night, and if they didn't say a lot, it was because they were too busy tossing clichés back and forth. I lost count of how many of them thought "outside the box" or had "gravitas", which sounded like "gravy" to me. They were in it for the gravy, that was for certain. I settled the issue by making Peter my chief of staff. I told him it was his job to fill the cabinet positions. Laurent approved, as delegation was the first skill a leader had to master. That was me. I was hellbent on being the best delegator who ever walked the hallowed halls of the white house.

While Peter was filling all those cabinet chairs, I was busy with more briefings than any person should be allowed to receive. The intelligence briefing came every morning, and it wasn't very "intelligent". How was I to remember where all the "stans" were? I mean, I knew they were in Asia…somewhere. So were China and Japan and Nepal, wherever that was. Mostly, I was concerned with domestic intelligence. If someone got blown up in a "stan", everything was just fine. If someone got blown up in Santa Barbara, it was a disaster. Luckily, I had the heads of the FBI and CIA on the job. They too smelled of swamp water, but that was the nature of the capital. You drag a billion dollars through the mud, and the critters come out. On the un-daily basis, I received briefings from the health agencies, the Social Security Administration, housing, commerce, the Treasury, Labor, and more bureaus than an English hotel. My brain was swimming in numbers and facts and datums and factoids. Most days, I couldn't remember if I had seen the ambassador from France or the ambassador from Belgium. Peter tried to keep my schedule in sync, but everyone wanted a minute with the president-elect. I had never been so popular, not even when I was the darling of the sitcoms.

But the pace was crushing.

I felt like a snow shovel seller the day before the blizzard hit. I didn't even have time to consult with my Advisors. And if that wasn't bad enough, Maria took that moment to join the cabinet within the cabinet.

Maria wasn't like the other Advisors. She didn't much care if I liked her. In fact, I had the distinct notion that she didn't want me to like her. Unlike the others, she told me when I was being an asshole (often) or a bitch (all the time). She didn't care about my feelings, which she considered rather pedestrian. To her way of thinking, everyone had feelings. In fact, everyone had exactly the same feelings. Some might have more of one than another. Or someone might feel a little deeper, but no one had a feeling no one had ever experienced before. So, feelings weren't worth a rat's ass, when it came to making decisions. In the greater scheme of things, they didn't separate one human from the next. Maria wasn't so sure feelings separated humans from dogs. She was pretty sure cats were on the outs, as cats didn't care about anything anyway. Maria was the Advisor who told me I was more than a little bit insane, and that I needed more help than I could afford to pay for. That really helped my old self-esteem. Luckily, the other Advisors pushed Maria to the background before she caused a Class-A breakdown.

If the briefings weren't enough, there was the whole inaugural thing.

I thought I made Peter the head of all things inaugural. But he was soon overwhelmed by the Cabinet wannabes, who dragged Peter into the swamp--the swamp consisting of long, alcohol-drenched lunches and a different cocktail party every night. The swamp was three parts alcohol and two parts lies. So, I had to deal with the ball planners and the dinner planners and the reception planners and the etiquette planners, because god forbid the Israeli ambassador was seated next to the Saudi Arabian ambassador. I wanted to skip the whole three days of folderol, but all the Advisors, except Maria, chanted the same word—"tradition". I was simply following the footsteps of the great presidents who came before me. That I couldn't name three of them made no difference. I was going have at least as many balls as the rest of them. I soon learned to pick up a phone the moment a "planner" appeared. A president-elect can fake phone calls because no one ever knows if there's a premier or dictator at the other end of the line. A born actress, I had no trouble carrying on fake conversations. When I saw the bill for my inauguration, I almost puked. We were spending those millions on what?

"Tradition."

I knew the answer before I asked the question.

The luckiest thing about the inauguration was that it was all superficial. It was play-acting. There were no problems to solve, no policies to formulate, no wars to start or end. It was nonstop smiles. It was leading the masses in our favorite chant…MAKE AMERICA WONDERFUL AGAIN. It was having a drink at every function, but only one, because there was always another function to attend. If anyone could pull off an inauguration week, it was America's Schoolgirl. I charmed the willing and the unwilling. I had a quip for every state, county, and city. I praised the capitals of every country on every continent. With a little help, I even said kinds words about the "stans". I was engaging and humble, but not too humble. I wasn't going to let some twerp from Europe look down at me.

I could settle his hash any time I felt like it. America wasn't the big kahuna for nothing.

After the last dance at the last ball, the last libation at the last bar, the Secret Service escorted me to the White House, the living quarters of the President of the United States of America. I had arrived. I was suddenly it, the it, the only it that really counted. The others could dance around and pretend, but I was it.

And I was terrified.

In my ball gown, in my bedroom, I sat on the bed and…cried.

What in god's name was I going to do?

Chapter 7

I didn't exactly spend the first real day of my presidency in bed. Technically, I was out of bed, even if I didn't leave my quarters. Technically, I did cry, as I knew I had bitten off quite a bit more than I could chew. My Advisors, minus Maria, assured me I would grow into the office. I would meet the challenge and then some. MAWA would rule the day. My natural instincts, such as they were, would pull me through.

My advisors, minus Maria, were idiots.

The only thing they got right was that I would rise and actually leave my room on day two. My new cabinet of warmed-over swamp rats smiled like actors at a photo shoot. Everyone waited for my pronouncements, for my leadership. I was to take us all to the heights I had promised during my campaign. What did "wonderful" really mean? I offered the pablum of the campaign. More of this and more of that and less of the other. They were with me because to be against me was to lose their job. I had promised the voters a reversal of the last administration, and that is what I set out to do. I promised a steady stream of executive decisions or orders or mandates or whatever they were called. I promised a drastic cut in rules and regulations. Who needed disease control anyway? If the Congress didn't want to work with me, I would go directly to the people. A GOFUNDME page would be enough for the armed forces, wouldn't it? At the end of the meeting, I led the cabinet in a prayer, calling on god to smite our enemies and put a chicken in every pot. I expected a quick call from Colonel Sanders, and I got it. Life was going to be a big bowl of cherries with whipped cream, something I ordered for dessert. I thought my first cabinet meeting was terrific. Why did the press call it a "disaster"?

After reading the papers and the Internet, Laurent suggested a world tour.

I couldn't have agreed more.

I had developed a taste for private jets, but they were dog meat compared to Air Force One. While the arrangements for my first trip were handled by the Secretary of State, a rather mousy, little woman with a left eye that twitched incessantly, something that would have distracted a blind person (how was I to focus while looking at that), preparing the jet was left to another planner or two. I commended the planners, as they provided for my every whim. It was as if I never left home. In fact, I was of a mind to simply stay on the plane and let the leaders of the world come to me, but the Advisors wouldn't allow that. Didn't I want to see the Eiffel Tower? So, the trip became rather monotonous. I would fly into one capital or another, meet with the movers and shakers, give a campaign speech to one large crowd or another, and hop back on Air Force One. If the crowds didn't always chant MAKE AMERICA WONDERFUL AGAIN, it was only because they didn't fully appreciate my vision. That I altered the vision with every stop didn't make it easy, but it was their job to keep up. One might have expected the Irish to embrace my crusade to end drinking in their country. They were such terrible singers, banning whiskey was the only way to save my ears.

Although the tour was fabulous and eye-opening, it soon flagged. How many state dinners with ethnic dancers could a president absorb? I made it through two-thirds of the trip before I decided it was time to go home. The Secretary of State's other eye began to twitch when I ordered Air Force One back to Washington. I had to give her credit for coming up with a rather unique excuse. She floated the rumor that I was pregnant. That made me laugh. As if old Peter could manage to arrange that. Of course, the bright pundits reasoned that America's Schoolgirl wasn't about to stretch out that old, tartan skirt, not for anything. And they were right. Still, it did bring a number of congratulatory emails from around the world, as well as a few condolences. There were some mothers who actually hated their little brats. I didn't blame them.

My first genuine crisis appeared upon landing at Andrews AFB. A group of university crybabies marched on the White House in an effort to save their precious food stamps, as if they needed them. One of my edicts or executive orders had altered the requirements slightly, making qualifying for food stamps a bit more difficult. I knew the silent majority was all for making food stamp recipients sing for their supper, metaphorically. And if the private sector couldn't engender a job for the leeches, then I would. I never promised anyone a "good" job. In fact, my Advisors said the worse the job, the quicker the parasites would move into the real economy. Who could argue with that? Wheelchairs and crutches be damned. They could all work.

Image.

That was what the Advisors worried about. How would things look?

I knew that I couldn't call up the National Guard to take truncheons to the pointy heads of those university brats. So, I simply asked for the defenders of liberty to protect the White House and its environs. I played to my base, and my base responded.

On the day of the march, the capital was filled with motorcycles, tractors, and pickups, more pickups than I thought existed. They all flew the flag, and more than a few sported beer-guzzling men with pistols strapped to their belts. They spit and cursed and laughed and drank, and in no time at all, chased those eggheads out of town. If a few heads got bashed in the process, well, not every tea party was quaint and dignified.

MAKE AMERICAN WONDERFUL AGAIN

They surrounded the reflecting pond and sang the anthem and set off fireworks, as if it was the Fourth of July. I could hardly have felt more proud of my fellow citizens. They reinforced my idea that food stamps were a privilege to be worked for, not a right. No one starved in my America, and if they did, my handlers tried to make it look like some kind of fake news. That was my catchall phrase. If I didn't like the headline, it was "fake news", pure and simple. Since most of my voters weren't strong on reading, I was pretty sure they would pick up my "fake news" cry and spread it far and wide. Fact checkers were, of course, my nemesis, so my minions harassed them out of existence. Seemed only fitting to me. The best thing about my unique solution to that first crisis was that the frat boys in the Che T-shirts stopped marching in my city. What a bonus.

Of course, there was a downside to solving a crisis. Once it was overcome, then the voters sat back and popped open another six pack. What kind of loyal following was that? My Advisors, minus Maria, recognized the problem right away. Without a constant stream of "solvable" crises, the MAWA crowd would grow more pudgy and lazy. Every fire needed stoking in January—or so someone used to say. The real crux of the issue was "solvable". I didn't want a crisis that overwhelmed me. I would overwhelm it. That was the real lesson of politics, as far as I as concerned.

Find a problem.

Make it sound like the end of the world.

Bring about overwhelming force.

Save the day.

What could go wrong?

I just needed a balloon of a problem that I could inflate to size of the Goodyear Blimp. It really wasn't that difficult. I looked out the window at the rose garden and figured it out in an instant.

"Buenos Dias."

CHAPTER 8

Had I studied the tiniest iota of history, I would have known that walls generally don't work. The Chinese tried it, and in the end had to give it up. Lots of medieval towns tried walls, only to discover that cannon balls beat stacked stones every time. If the force was strong enough, the wall fell. I knew there was something about Jericho I was supposed to remember, but that didn't matter. While looking at the garden, I had discovered the crisis I needed. There were too many immigrants swarming across the border with Mexico. And to my way of thinking, or rather, to my voters' way of thinking, a wall was absolutely necessary.

When I called for a wall at the next MAWA rally, the crowd went into a frenzy. I could tell by the "Amens" and "Hallelujahs" that I had struck a nerve. A wall from the Gulf of Mexico the Pacific Ocean was exactly what the people wanted. A tall wall with guard towers every quarter mile, towers armed by snipers and machine guns. The wall needed to be electrified, so that not even a toddler could wander through. Spotlights for night shooting and motion detectors for those foggy times when sight was curtailed. When I threw out the idea of a mine field on the Mexican side of the wall, the crowd became euphoric. I was the promised one leading them into salvation. I thought a moat was overkill, but by then, the mob was ready to drive to the border and park every fifty feet, staying there until the wall replaced them. After the rally, when a fake news reporter asked me about the wall, I reminded him of all the jobs the wall would create for sharpshooters and undertakers. American work would be done by Americans. I was surprised the reporter didn't get that. No doubt he was part of the liberal backbiters that my voters chased out of their perfect little towns.

While the wall provided continuing benefits, I stumbled a bit when I tried to pick a fight with Malta. I didn't know much about Malta, but I knew something about picking the right enemy. Dad had always told me that the way to win a fight was to pick a weak enemy, attack with overwhelming force, and offer generous peace terms. Malta seemed like the perfect setup. Tiny, weak, I figured the 101st Airborne could occupy the island in a few hours. They would have too, if some leaker in the Pentagon hadn't tipped off the purveyors of fake news. Luckily, I was able to put the blame on some liberal generals I wanted to can anyway. They protested, but my peeps knew the libs always protested when they were caught blue-handed.

I was feeling pretty proud of myself, and then some idiot artist turned MAWA into MAKE AMERICA WACK-OFF AGAIN. That mural on a DC street was the icing on the cake, so to speak. I had enough of the artiste class making fun of me and my voters. Little did they know that I controlled the purse strings. That money that went to the endowment for the arts, suddenly disappeared. The funding for those pesky community organizers dried up like a shallow puddle under the noon sun. If they wanted to make fun of me, they would pay the price. America's Schoolgirl had learned a little something over the years. If I could have done more with other countries, I would have been happier. Sure, I could smack their hands before they took the cookies, but they weren't beholding to me. They had their own money…damn them. Still, as the year wound down, I was feeling almost good. If the swamp things in the cabinet kept asking for more, well, that was their job. I had ways to settle with their constant carping.

Year two began with dad's well-tested way to relieve pressure. It was called the cigar connection. By that, dad meant you had to smoke cigars back to back to back. He preferred cigars, because he didn't inhale cigars. Neither did I, and I had to admit a good Cuban cigar hit the spot after a MAWA rally. I had the Secret Service change the bands on the cigars, so everyone thought I was smoking Virginia cigars, as if anyone would ever smoke those. I had to wear a glove when I smoked so no one would see nicotine-stained fingers. The sacrifices I made for my image.

The problem with any vice is that the effects lessen with time. One cigar becomes half a dozen and one bourbon becomes a bottle. I didn't want to invest in mouthwash, so I decided to try a new vice. It was simple really. The drug enforcement people picked up the Columbian drug lord. I laid out the deal, and he jumped at the chance to supply the White House with primo, full-strength cocaine. Sure, I had to use a Secret Service agent to test a batch when it arrived, but they didn't complain too much. It was eight hours of nirvana. I was positively the best prez the service had ever protected. When a bad batch arrived, the drug lord lost a finger. He was definitely not into rings.

It was at that moment that I decided to finish the world tour I had cut short after the inauguration. The Secretary of State's eyes twitched constantly as we put more than a few miles on Air Force One. And I had to admit that the cocaine habit was a lot less messy than the cigar one. The best part of the trip was that I didn't remember a lot of it. That's the beauty of being high. Those nasty little details are relegated to the memory dump. I must have been just fine, because the Secretary of State started drinking to excess half way through the tour. Why would she do that if I wasn't performing just fine?

In fact, my performance must have been laudatory.

The stock market set a new high almost every week.

The tech masters of the universe said nothing but good things about me.

If the people in the hinterlands were running a bit behind on the rent, well, they could get food stamps—as long as they were willing to work.

My invent-a-crisis management allowed me to foist the ills of the country onto the backs of the elite swamp rats and liberal oddballs. My loyal voters believed every word I pronounced, even the ones I had to repeat three times before they understood. My world wasn't perfect, but it was manageable, as long as the drug lord didn't skimp on the white powder. With two years under my belt, the Advisors started looking toward the next election, which was fine with me. The electoral college was my friend. My MAWA rallies would be SRO. I was waving goodbye to the idiots of the left who thought they could keep up.

Two years to go.

What could go wrong?

I was about to find out.

Chapter 9

Who would have thought that "chubo" would cause a problem? I mean, it wasn't as if the leader of North Korea was svelte. He was a rather obnoxious, round, short man who insisted on blowing his cigarette-laced breath into my face. I was the President. No one blew smoke in my face, or up my skirt. Chubo needed to learn that. Still, the truth did hurt a few feelings. Chubo raised a ruckus, and the Chinese sang the chorus, and before I knew it, people were predicting war. It was batshit crazy, but I had come to expect that from the munchkins who wanted to bring down the US of A. So, when the Chinese premier called to ask me to apologize, I told him to call his Nork buddy and get him to apologize. I might have carried on a bit too long and not used the proper title, but hey, I wasn't the one living a lie. Well, I was, but my lie wasn't the topic of moment. Chubo's fat was the topic, and I was right.

That was when twitchy-eyes took over and mollified everyone—except for Chubo, of course. He, supposedly, had his chubby little finger on the launch button. But I didn't care. If he wanted to start tossing missiles, I would see his Sam-Dong, or whatever and raise him a few Minutemen. Chubo learned the error of his ways. All it cost me were a few tons of rice for his starving country.

But the Norks weren't the only ones who got their knickers in a bunch over the slightest things. The whole Middle East was filled with men who saw disrespect in every little phrase. Like "raghead" hadn't already been around the globe about a million times. Was I supposed to call them that? No, and I didn't in private. But it was a MAWA rally, and the good old boys with the NRA tattoos needed something to shout about. So, I tossed out the nick, and the crowd exploded. I thought the emirs and sultans and whatever would understand that "raghead" was the moral equivalent of "death to America". In fact, I was pretty sure "death to America" was a whole lot worse. Did I rant and rave when they shouted that to their fanatics? No, I understood it was all stagecraft. It was how we worked the crowd. The press went ballistic, as expected. I had just committed the faux pas of the century. No doubt the strait of harmony, or whatever it was, would be closed, and half the world would have to peddle bicycles to work. The press could turn unconditional victory into some sort of hidden defeat. Not that it mattered much. When the Middle East didn't burst into flames, I told the crowds it was nothing but more "fake news".

About that time, twitchy-eyes had a break down. I didn't see it, but the Secret Service boys caught her trying to sneak an UZI into a cabinet meeting. She claimed it was meant for me, as if I needed an UZI. She was screaming when she was taken away. No doubt, the little dust up with the emirs had been too much for her.

Of course, that left the Secretary of State job open, and boy, did the swamp critters come sniffing after that. I knew that it was a plum job. In effect, it was a twelve-month holiday. Jump on a plane and throw a dart at a map. The Secretary of State was never home. When they weren't escorting the President from capital to capital, they were negotiating a cease fire or trade deal. That the cease fire never lasted more than thirty minutes, or that the trade deal cost the US a few million jobs didn't seem to make a dent in anyone's thinking. The Sec of State had negotiated something. Strike up the band.

I wanted to name someone right away, and I did. The problem was the Senate. Peter read me the pertinent clause from the Constitution, that little thing about advise and consent. As far as I was concerned, the Senate's job was to pretty much give me the person I wanted. I didn't see where grilling the candidate for a day or two would do anyone any good. I told the MAWA crowds that very thing, and they cheered. Why did a bunch of overpaid President-wannabes think they had the right to derail my nominations? The Advisors, minus Maria, told me to play nice with the Senators. They had my back for the most part. Letting them look presidential during some hearings wasn't too much to ask. I pointed out that the high and haughty had given me twitchy-eyes of UZI fame. If they had blown that one, they might well blow another. Still, I took their advice. The Senate could hold their hearings and hear themselves take three minutes to ask the nominee what time it was. I could abide that. It was the Supreme Court that was turning out to be the thorn in my paw.

I fully understood the theory of the Supreme Court. Nine old people in black robes held a tribunal of sorts where people came to argue the finer points of the law. These sages then went back to their offices and consulted their chicken entrails or Ouija boards or whatever they used to get the answer they wanted. If they needed a penumbra, they found one hiding behind some article of the constitution. If the clear language of a law or statute or article of the constitution didn't give them what they wanted, they deemed the language antiquated or too vague or not germane to the technology of the day. They had turned twisted words into an art form. They discovered "rights" no one at the constitutional convention had ever heard of, let alone written about. And the absolute worst part of the Supremes was that their word was final. No appeal to a higher court, no two out three, no sleep on it. They were as serious as a heart attack and a lot more final. It was maddening.

I knew it was maddening, because the MAWA crowds agreed with me about SCOTUS. And the MAWA crowds were rarely wrong.

You would think the Supremes would heed the will of the people, as expressed through me, but that would be too much to ask. They weren't elected. I was. And they served for life. Even as they doddered about, falling asleep half the time during oral arguments, they still couldn't be kicked off the court. I knew there were suggestions to add more black robes to the court, say another 50 or so. As long as it was an odd number, you could get a majority. But the Advisors, minus Maria, voted against court packing. If America's Schoolgirl couldn't sway nine, how was I going to sway fifty-nine? They were right. I was just going to have to live with it. I considered giving twitchy-eyes her UZI back and handing her a list of addresses, but that felt like bad form. Besides, if I needed to go that route, I could always get some MAWA boys to do the trick.

Relying on cocaine and cigars (and a dollop of bourbon), I managed to stay one step ahead of the Supremes, or one lap behind. I wasn't sure. In any case, I was nearing the end of year three, and I realize I had another election to win. I was ready—

most days. My well-oiled campaign organization was set. I didn't care who was running against me. I was ready.

The problem was, my Advisors weren't.

Chapter 10

Someone once told me that rule by committee can never work. There is no way to please everyone, and if everyone compromises, then the result is something as tepid and rancid as swamp water. I had never subscribed to that view, but I was learning that it was true. The Advisors were no longer on the same page. Hell, they weren't even in the same book, maybe not even the same library. Every one of them, with the exception of Maria, had been coopted by an agenda. Every one of them had become the puppet of some faction, half of which I didn't even recognize. Who were the brethren of anarchy anyway? One Advisor talked prison camps. Another touted the National Guard. A third sang the praises of Martial Law. A fourth danced to the tune of dictatorship. While they might have had a common theme, they were wildly different.

Then, there was Maria.

Maria was the sanity fighting a losing battle against insanity. After all, insanity was vastly more appealing than sanity. Anyone could be sane. But insanity was an art form. Insanity called for creativity and imbalance. Insanity was a goal and a shield. What could anyone do to an insane person? That was the beauty of being off one's rocker. The worst they could do was feed you a steady diet of happy pills, that you didn't even have to take! What a scam. Want to create a little havoc? Go off the meds and do your worst. A slap on the wrist and back on the meds—till life got too boring again. Simple, almost elegant. And everyone thought they were helping.

Then, there was Maria.

She understood the scam. She fought for sanity and truth and right thinking. She fought for boredom, which was the eighth deadly sin and trumped all the others. Thou shalt not be bored. It was written in stone some place. To escape the sin of boredom, anything was allowed. If you happened to be Prez, then that "anything" included actions no one else on earth could match. Find yourself lazing away a perfectly fine Sunday afternoon? Start a small war. A few thousand killed here and there weren't even a blip on the screen. Movies might be great for simulated explosions, but there was nothing like the real thing. And the drones provided spectacular footage. Beat the hell out of the NFL. That as child's play.

Then, there was Maria.

Maria was against those small wars. She was for the poor. She wanted everyone to eat and sleep under a roof and not die of an infected hangnail. She thought everyone deserved some spending money and the chance to become better than they were. She believed people needed to share and help. She wanted people to forego their weekly injection of TV and drugs. People needed to garden and teach and sing together in a common cause.

Boring, boring, boring, boring.

Maria's boring voice was swamped by the chorus of voices that demanded their own little version of excitement. The Advisors had become excitement junkies. They wanted more.

That was the trouble with excitement. Unlike boredom, which didn't come in degrees, which didn't inure the soul, excitement was a drug that people soon became immune to. Like the fabulous cocaine I was using, excitement required bigger and bigger doses in order to achieve the same level of joy. What excited this morning wouldn't excite in the afternoon and would be positively boring by evening. Simulations became tedious. Who wanted to watch a film when real gore could be produced? Who wanted video of a riot in Rio, when downtown Portland was around the corner? Portland too small? How about Chicago? The tinkle of shattering glass was only a nightfall away. Excitement. The ultimate addiction. The monster that had to be fed daily. Because without constant feeding, boredom conquered all.

Boredom.

To be avoided at all costs.

Except by Maria.

In order to avoid the curse of boredom, I took to cocaine doses so large, I had to avoid a lot of daily interaction. Peter and the swamp critters made excuses for me. While I still held the occasional MAWA rally, I found them incredibly boring. How many times can you hear "four more years" before it becomes trite and banal? The excitement of ten thousand throaty roars was gone. Heard it, been there, got the seven, different, road show T-shirts. In my quarters, in that nether world of drug addiction, I could find excitement once again. A cruise missile here, a drone strike there, a peaceful protest disbanded by a cadre of truncheon-bearing police, there was excitement galore—under the right circumstances. I couldn't wallow in the excitement, though. When the swamp critters were left on their own, all manner of havoc ensued.

Like food stamps.

I thought I had fixed that problem once and for all, but every time I turned my back, the head of the program and his army of lawyers would sneak in a new exception to my ironclad rules. Since I was intimately acquainted with the insanity game, I didn't buy the mental illness gambit. Everyone had the meds they needed to work. If they went off their meds, they weren't suddenly qualified for food stamps. That was true insanity. They made a choice, a bad choice, and bad choices weren't things to be rewarded. How in the name of Sigmund Freud did anyone learn anything if their terrible decisions brought no consequences? Every child understood the paddle. Every lune who jettisoned their meds needed the lesson of hunger. Hunger made those meds mighty attractive.

And it wasn't just food stamps. I had to stomp out fires all through the government. Worse, I had to put out the fires while trying to placate the Supremes. They were forever meddling in the affairs of the bureaucracy. They needed to be taught a lesson also, but I couldn't very well send them to a reeducation camp, despite what the Advisors, minus Maria, counseled. Luckily, the US Marshall Service worked for me and not them. I did think about letting the brethren of anarchy torch the Supreme Court building. All it would take was a stand down order. But Maria convinced me that real fire wasn't needed. A CGI of the building in flames in an email would work just as well. It did, and it didn't. The Supremes were not ones to give up easily. It wasn't as if I could threaten their jobs, and most of them didn't have young children anymore. I was stuck.

That was when boredom raised its ugly mug. To vanquish that foe, I turned on the news. I listened to Britain's Prime Minister, and my blood boiled.

Chapter 11

The most charming and devastating aspect of the British is their accent. They manage to make rather awful insults sound endearing. But the Prime Minister's accent couldn't hide his abject disdain for American leadership—me. I didn't need an interpreter to know that I had been dissed. It was a diss with a smile and wit, but it was a diss. And according to the rules of the hood, I had to do something about the diss.

So, I called a meeting of the staff.

Without the staff.

The oval office was crowded with the Advisors. I was pretty sure my secretary had her ear to door, listening to the one-sided conversation, as the Advisors spoke inside my head. I doubted that my half was elucidating. Not that it mattered. Lots of people talked to themselves. Not many had a full chorus inside their heads.

They stepped up in order, Laurent first. He recounted history, how the Founding Fathers didn't stand for any British guff. The others took their turn, adding their anger over being dissed. That was what bullies did, and there was but one way to deal with a bully. Maria tried to say something, but she was drowned out by the others. Arthur said it was perfectly logical to defend one's honor. The sentiment was running in one direction. Then, the Matron commanded the floor. Her take was

I wasn't quite sure how to take things. Deep inside, I had the feeling that starting a war over words was rather silly. Yet, I needed to do something. A snort of cocaine was in order.

That brought out the Matron, who was not happy to be summoned.

"Are you sorry?" I asked.

"For what?" The Matron wasn't in the mood for niceties.

"For treating me like some kind of baggage when I was kid. I had needs. I was all alone. It was you that made me into what I am. And let's not mince words about what I have become."

"I'm not sorry. Grow up."

That was when I lost it. That was when my anger burst forth. I would show her. I would show all of them. I started sending tweets, and I started cursing, and I was yelling like a banshee at a wake. I was the greatest president the greatest country in the world had ever elected. I would not stand idly by and let the liberal media sing the praises of some English twit. I was going to do something. I was going to make people pay. I had been more than a bit abused. I needed to strike back. I was screaming, working myself into a lather. I would make them all pay!

I must have been louder than I intended, because at some point in my rant, the door burst open. Peter came running in with several Secret Service agents. They must have thought I was under attack (I was), because they had their guns out. I wasn't quite sure about everything else that happened. Peter led me out of the oval office and straight to my bedroom. He said I needed "rest". He meant I needed to dry out. That was reasonable, well, not so much.

simple. No American President would abide the disrespect o[f a] British clown. I suggested a mean Twitter post, but the Matr[on] would have none of that. If I wanted respect, I would have [to] do something special. After all, if I tolerated the PM, then [I] would have to tolerate every third world dictator with a phon[e.] The Resolute desk demanded something resolute. I had to sen[d] a message…all caps.

BRIT PM CLOWN HAIR CHARLIE. APOLOGIZE O[R] PREPARE FOR A SECOND REVOLUTIONARY WAR. AMERICA HAS A STRONG, STABLE ECONOMY, PROUD BORDER, AND HARD-WORKING PEOPLE. YOU DON'T WANT TO MESS WITH US. APOLOGIZE!

One didn't have to be a prophet to guess how the media would take the message. The haters saw it as proof of presidential insanity. No one threatened an ally with war. The media on my side called the note a bastion for American values. The dispute raged, until the PM said he never meant to insult America or its President. His comments echoed the global take on the current style and substance of American leadership. Nothing personal.

That sounded like bullcrap to Laurent, who said the Brit[s] and the rest of the world needed a lesson in humility. A bit of drone here or there might teach everyone that America too[k] insults seriously. Arthur pointed out that a war gained us nothing. And certainly, the Brits would have to retaliate. Lauren[t] assured me that it was only a war if the other side had a chanc[e] of winning. Since the Brits had no chance, a few explosion[s] would be little more than a show of dominance. I had absorbe[d] a good many insults over the years, and I had had enoug[h.] America's Schoolgirl was growing into America's bitch.

And I did dry out, sort of. I found cartoons soothing, but not as soothing as static. I mean, I found a certain peace in the dots, the pulsing dots and toneless static of the TV. It was odd, weird, but it was true. The static spoke to me in ways the cartoon couldn't. In ways, the Advisors couldn't. I suppose it was a kind of meditation. I could lose myself in the space where nothing was. I was happily lost in the monotone, when Peter came in.

Peter didn't mince words. He came straight out and said he was going to leave. Not permanently, not forever, just for a week or two. He needed to clear his head. H told me I could go with him. He was going to fish and commune with nature. I wasn't much of a fisherwoman; I never even baited the hook. Fishing definitely did not appeal to me. If I wasn't going fishing, I needed to clear my head and get back to work. Peter said the world was begging for sound leadership, and the President was the person everyone turned to. If I didn't climb back in the saddle forthwith, the twitter universe would cancel me. I didn't think it was that bad, but he had a point. I couldn't wallow in static forever. He told me who was going to be in charge in his absence, and that was fine with me. Off he went. I let him. I had other plans.

The next morning, I dressed in camo, one of my favorite outfits. I smiled my way past the stares and gapes and walked into the oval office. I had the beginning of a plan in my head, but I needed something more. The temporary chief of staff and half the white house minions piled into the office. It seemed no one had made a decision since I went to my room. No mind. I turned on the TV to the conservative news station and listened as the talking heads bemoaned how the awful liberals were treating America's Schoolgirl. I sent my chief of staff for a diet coke and cleared the room of everyone else. I needed to think. When the chief came back with the drink, I told him to call the Pentagon. I wanted the joint chiefs in the situation room in one hour. There was serious business to attend to. I was the President to do it.

The world wouldn't know what hit them.

Chapter 12

The situation room was filled with gold bars and stars and dour-faced men and women who didn't quite understand what I as saying. I thought my plan both simple and brilliant. We would launch drone attacks against England, but not against the English people. Oh no, we didn't want to kill people. We simply wanted to wipe out enough infrastructure to cause the Brits to surrender. The first wave would take out all the military bases and communication facilities. Modern armies lived on information. We would deny them information first. Then, we would take out the power grid. Nothing works without power. And the Brits sure as hell didn't have enough batteries to go around. I smiled around the table. What did they think?

Not much.

That was the consensus of the joint chiefs. They couldn't fathom going to war with Britain and, perhaps, all of Europe over the diss. I pointed out that it wasn't just the diss. A quick strike would send a vital message to any and all potential enemies. You diss us, and we take you back to the ice age. Wasn't an ounce of prevention worth a pound of cure? I couldn't understand their reluctance.

Especially, after the vice president weighed in.

The VP, a god-fearing evangelical, backed me to the hilt. In his words, the commies and Arabs would think twice before they ran off at the mouth. And if they dared try terrorism we would bomb them till there weren't two bricks to stack on one another. I appreciated the VP's support, but it still wasn't enough to sway the joint chiefs. That's when I decided that the chiefs served at the pleasure of the President, and this President was not pleased.

That began the slaughter. In a matter of minutes, I had the resignations of the entire joint chiefs. No problem. They marched out, as if they couldn't be replaced. Nothing was further from the truth. It took me some hours, but I managed to appoint a new cadre of promotable warriors, young Turks who saw the world through my glasses. They jumped into planning with enthusiasm. If my stand-in chief of staff wasn't so gung-ho, well, that was the way it had to be. We were having a great time trying to decide if Big Ben could be considered a communication device. If it was, we would bomb it. The younger generals thought that would be cool. I wasn't sold on the idea, but watching the tower fall would be a great message. Nothing was sacred, as far as America's Schoolgirl was concerned. It would be Busted Ben by the end of the day.

I didn't notice my temporary chief of staff go to the door. I didn't notice the VP join him. I did notice when the door opened, and a SWAT team rushed in. That was when the VP and chief of staff started yelling "Twenty-fifth Amendment", as if I was supposed to know what that said. I tried to rally the troops, but my newly anointed joint chiefs did absolutely nothing. They were led out like lambs, even as the VP jumped on the comm and recalled all those beautiful drones I had launched. If I hadn't been handcuffed, I would have beaten the

VP to a pulp. Instead, I was led out by the men in black masks and deposited in my own bedroom. Restraints bound me to the bed, and my long recovery began. Despite the fact that I screamed bloody murder and demanded to be turned loose, no one did a thing. My reign as President had come to a screeching halt.

What came next were the lost weeks. I didn't remember much about them. There were periods of consciousness when I ate and chatted with a therapist that reminded me of Frankenstein. He was, no doubt, the ugliest man I had ever met, and thus pretty much immune to the disease known as America's Schoolgirl. I didn't talk to him. I didn't need to. I was the President. If I was slightly out of commission at the moment, that would soon end. The rest of the time, I was pretty much asleep.

But I did get better.

The Advisors, plus Maria, went into hibernation. Without the constant war of words, I was able to make contact with the real world. I became so lucid, the chief of staff brought me out for the annual Easter Egg Hunt. I stood to the side, smiling, as the urchins raced around for eggs. I was thankful for the sunlight. In my own way, I posed for photos. I knew the Internet would soon be swimming with shots of me, all well. Hah! Little did they know. I made it through the hunt and returned to my bedroom. That was when the chief of staff informed me that I had won a bunch of primaries and was going to lead the ticket in November. That was insane, but that was how my voters were. They wanted me no matter what. If I never went campaigning, I stood a good chance of winning a second term.

Yay.

Peter returned. He said my campaign was running well, but I needed to get myself ready for some rallies, if I needed them. In order to do that, I had to spill my guts to the new therapist, who was a slight improvement over Frankenstein. I did, although I didn't tell the truth. I had been lying for so long, I couldn't separate the truth from the lies. My parents had been from the planet Morg, hadn't they? In any case, the therapist certified me as sane, and that was all it took. The campaign took that and ran. I smiled my way through two Sunday morning interviews, where I knew the questions ahead of time. And that was it. By election day, I had not held a rally or engaged in a debate. I was almost a recluse, and yet, I was in the race. Was America a great country or what?

That night, I watched the returns with Peter in the oval office. While the VP and others bit their lips as the results came in, I found myself quite at ease. I hadn't been so calm since my days with cocaine. As the results piled up, I fell behind. Then, later, as most states reported, I pulled even, or nearly so. It was close, very close. The others in the room grew quiet. I sipped a diet coke and stared at the TV that was slowly coming apart. No, the TV wasn't coming apart, the picture was. My eyes were seeing past the talking heads who were about to call the election. My eyes slipped right on by, right to the static, that beautiful static that was behind all the other stuff. I listened as the chief talking head told the audience that they could now call a winner. The election was over.

I

Had

Found

My

Place

In the static, the peaceful static.

I would never return.

THE END

www.ingramcontent.com/pod-product-compliance
Lightning Source LLC
Chambersburg PA
CBHW020035120526
44588CB00031B/807